Maneuver and Dock Your Sailboat Under Power

Maneuver and Dock Your Sailboat Under Power

HIGH WINDS, CURRENT, TIGHT MARINA, BACKING IN? NO PROBLEMS!

GRANT HEADIFEN

Seahorse Publishing

Dedication

To all those poor souls who have arrived at the marina to find a strange and mysterious new scratch in their gorgeous gelcoat. May your boat rest in peace. And, if you ever find out who it was, harbor no bad thoughts—just send them a copy of this book.

Acknowledgments

Many of the photos in this book are courtesy of Beneteau.

Seahorse Publishing books may be purchased in bulk at special discounts for sales promotion, corporate gifts, fund-raising, or educational purposes. Special editions can also be created to specifications. For details, contact the Special Sales Department, Skyhorse Publishing, 307 West 36th Street, 11th Floor, New York, NY 10018 or info@skyhorsepublishing.com.

Seahorse® and Seahorse Publishing® are registered trademarks of Skyhorse Publishing, Inc.®, a Delaware corporation.

Visit our website at www.skyhorsepublishing.com.

10 9 8 7 6 5

Library of Congress Cataloging-in-Publication Data is available on file.

Cover design by Tom Lau
Cover photo credit Annapolis Yacht Sales

Print ISBN: 978-1-944824-06-8

Printed in the United States of America

Contents

Introduction

How This Book Works

This book is unlike any other book you've read. We call it a hybrid eBook. While the book can stand on its own as one of the best learn-to-sail books ever written, it also employs some really cool technology should you decide to take advantage.

Throughout the book, you will see QR codes. When you scan these codes with your mobile device, the book will come alive and present interactive animations, videos, and useful websites. This will vastly enhance your learning experience.

To get a QR code reader, simply search any app store. QR code readers are free. Alternatively, NauticEd provides a free iOS app that can read QR codes. You can go to www.NauticEd.org/sailing-apps and download the free app there. Once you have it downloaded, click on the hybrid eBook link in the App menu.

Try out your QR code reader now and go to the webpage www.NauticEd.org/book-maneuvering for this book where we show an introductory video, all the links used for this book, and any updates post-publication.

NauticEd is one of the world's leading sailing training companies and the only company to employ super-high-technology systems in its training programs. NauticEd also helps students gain the ICC, or International Certificate of Competence. The ICC was created by the United Nations and is required as a sailing license in many countries. Yacht charter companies worldwide accept the NauticEd sailing resume and certification system.

This book is not only going to be part of your world-class sailing training but it will lead you to a highly regarded sailing certification that is accepted globally.

As part of your purchase of this book, you will have free access to a lot of tools that are introduced here. By simply scanning the QR codes, a new world of modern sailing training, sailing resumes, sailing logbooks, and sailing badges will be opened to you—*all for free.*

About This Course

Maneuvering a sailboat under power is one of the most overlooked skills. It is a skill that absolutely must be learned. When sailing in open waters it's reasonably difficult to hit something as long as you have a proper watch out, and radar and navigation skills. When maneuvering around in the marina it's reasonably easy and common to hit something—namely, the dock or other boats. And, of course, hitting either is expensive and embarrassing.

My Own Start

Near the beginning of my open-water sailing career, I chartered a 46-foot sailboat in St. Maarten, where the charter base is in a protected cove with a tricky reef entrance. Because of the entrance, the charter base requires that a pilot come out to your boat in a speedboat, jump on board and bring the boat through the reef, and park it in the slip in the marina for you. I spent some time observing this very talented Rastafarian expertly maneuver my chartered boat into the slip.

It was a maneuvering job with which I was very impressed. Why? Well, just days before I had wiped the BBQ off from the back of my sailboat because I could not maneuver the boat in a tight marina with 20 knots of side wind just as it was getting dark. I had been trying to back up to a concrete wall and simultaneously lasso pilings as they went past to hold the front of the boat in place and—off the wall. As captain, I was seeing very quickly that my open water experience was not paying off and was about to cost me, the charter company, and the insurance company a lot of money. Luckily, the expense turned out to be just the BBQ clamp.

I remember a year later maneuvering a 50-foot Beneteau sailboat into the marina in the beautiful port of Bonifacio, Corsica. Our slip was right next to a sidewalk restaurant loaded with tourists, so it was imperative to my ego to get it right. Well, I did, but actually I think it was really more luck than anything else. As we sat on the back of the boat celebrating a no-damage docking, we watched a crew expertly maneuver their boat backwards down a row of slips, then turn right angles, then back their boat into a tight slip, stopping perfectly. We all cheered and clapped as it was very impressive. I vowed right then and there to learn the skill.

One year later I was smiling as I maneuvered a 50-foot sailboat through a very tight harbor in Kos, Greece. You can always tell how you are doing in a busy port. If you're doing well, everyone on the other boats will be watching and will continue to drink their gin. If you're doing badly, they all put down their drinks and put fenders over the side. In Greece, everyone continued drinking!

This book will teach you how to practice and master the skill of placing the boat however and wherever you want it every time, in all wind situations, with confidence. The lessons here are arranged so you can first read the material and begin to understand the theory. Then you can practice. Each chapter has associated practical exercises that you absolutely must perform and repeat to become an expert. The exercises are designed to get you extremely comfortable with maneuvering your boat.

At the end, I'm confident that you'll be so comfortable with maneuvering and backing your boat in a tight marina that you'll never have any onlookers need to put down their drink and pick up a fender. You'll feel great and, even if you mess it up a bit, you'll know exactly how to do it better next time.

After going through this material, we recommend taking this book, a friend, some sandwiches, and some non-alcoholic libations with you to the boat. Then have a great day performing all the practical exercises on the water several times over to master the concepts.

Watch this video of us doing figure 8's out on the water. It was fun!

Please enjoy yourself and our lessons, brought to you by Captain Grant Headifen, USCG Master Mariner and Global Director of Education for NauticEd.

Chapter 1
Momentum

Throughout this book, we will explain the concept and combine it with real exercises that we will have you perform on a real boat. For now, however, we want you to work all the way through the book just imagining yourself on the boat to fully grasp the concepts in your mind. At the end of the course is a printable document that you will take to your boat in order to really do the exercises. At that stage, you will have embedded in your mind a superior knowledge of what to expect.

Through years of teaching this course, we have found this creates the best learning process for you. Here is your first real practical exercise for you to imagine for now.

Exercise 1: Under power and going down wind, move towards one of the buoys and stop the boat with the buoy abeam of the boat. You'll invariably overshoot. No problem, though, because you're in deep water and nowhere near a marina.

What you learned: You overshot for two reasons: the boat has a massive amount of momentum, and the wind is pushing you from behind. To do it better next time, put the engine into reverse about 5 boat lengths back at about 1000 rpm. As the boat begins to slow, gauge whether you should increase the engine speed against the approaching speed of the buoy. Work the engine up to 2500 rpm and down to ensure you stop in the desired place. Most people make the mistake of putting the engine in reverse too late, then having to overpower the engine at the last minute.

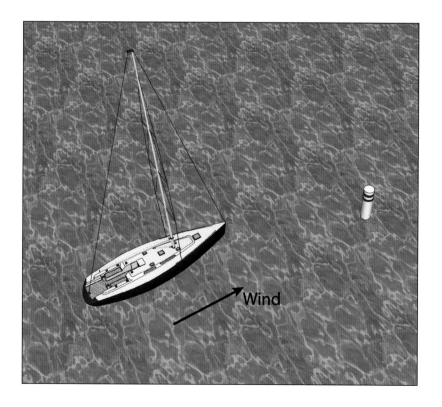

Exercise 2: Repeat exercise 1, but headed into the wind.

What you learned: You still run the possibility of overshooting your mark largely because of the momentum of the boat. The exact same principles apply. Use reverse with plenty of space, and work the engine to gauge your approach.

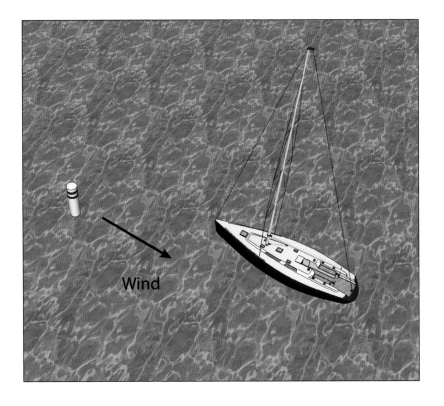

Wind

The bottom line here is that the boat does not work very well in reverse. As another example from standing still, notice the acceleration of the boat in both forward and reverse. You'll see that the boat takes off much faster in forward. That's easy—because the propeller is mostly used in forward, the shape of the prop is engineered to have its greatest efficiency in forward. The tradeoff is poor performance in reverse. However, enter the innovative reversing propeller. The following video shows a reversing propeller turning and then flipping its blades entirely around so that the blades always work in their most efficient mode.

This video is courtesy of MaxProp, who manufacture the reversing prop.

Chapter 2
Maneuvering in Forward

Exercise 3: Position the boat abeam of a buoy and about half a boat length away. Check for traffic! Now put the wheel hard over and do 5 donuts around the buoy at 2500 rpm. Yipee!

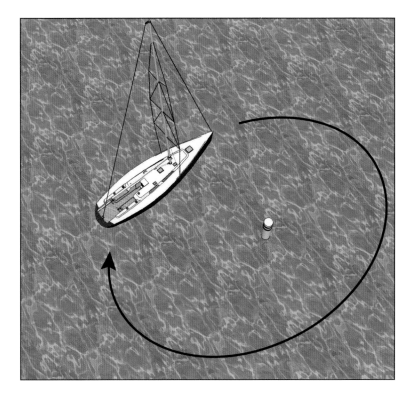

What you learned: You'll see that the boat turns in an extremely tight circle, not much larger than the length of the boat. You'll see that on a windy day the track of the boat is not affected by the wind. Now do the same at 1000 rpm. Especially on a windy day, you'll notice that the circle diameter is larger and you have much less turning control.

Note

Water flowing past the rudder gives you control of the boat. The more water flow, the more control. When the prop is pushing water over the rudder, the effect is additive—that is, you have water flow from the boat speed and water flow from the propeller. The downside effect of the propeller pushing water over the rudder is that you continue to gain boat speed, which is not what you want in a marina.

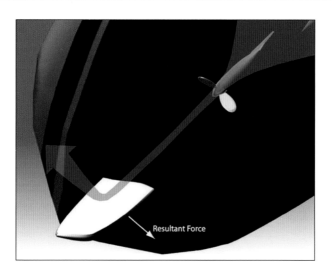

Exercise 4: With the boat laying still, pointing down wind and engine in neutral, first turn the wheel hard over and increase the engine in forward to 2500 rpm for 2 seconds, then back to 1000 rpm.

What you learned: You'll see that the boat turns very fast but does not gain any appreciable forward speed. Try the same exercise but only rev the engine to 1000 rpm max. You'll see that the boat does not turn as fast and, in fact, on a windy day you may not be able to turn the boat up into the wind at all. If there was a boat in front of you, you'd probably hit it. Revving the engine for 2 seconds shoots a wash of water over the rudder to give you a burst of control. This method should be used in most situations to gain greater control of the boat.

Exercise 5: To gain an appreciation of control of the boat, do figure 8's around 2 buoys that are spaced close to each other—or just use some imaginary buoys. As you begin the turn, rev the engine to 2500 rpm and then back down to 1500 as you come out of the turn and straighten up to approach the next buoy.

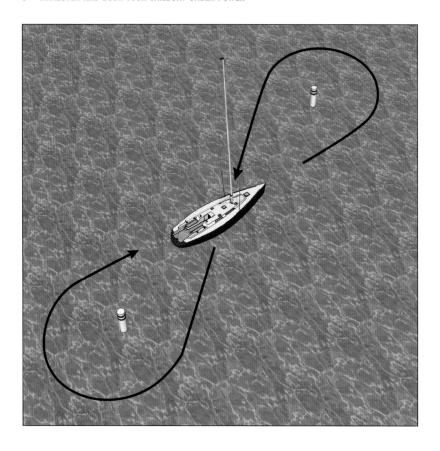

What you learned: The simple series of exercises will give you a good feeling on how to maneuver and control the boat in forward gear.

Exercise 6: Pretend you are going to maneuver into a slip as follows. Use the buoy and imagine the slip. You have heavy downwind.

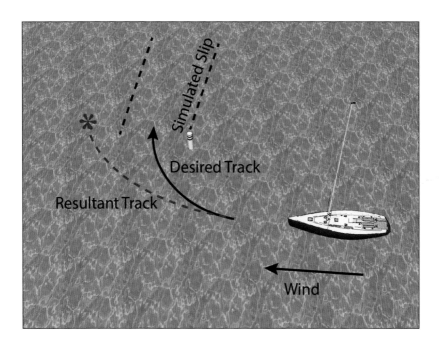

What you learned: You'll probably overshoot on the resultant track and cause some pretty big damage because the momentum of the boat with the force of the wind will carry you past your intended track. Instead you'll find that the boat is much more stable if it is driving into the wind when in forward. Therefore, try the exercise again using the following method.

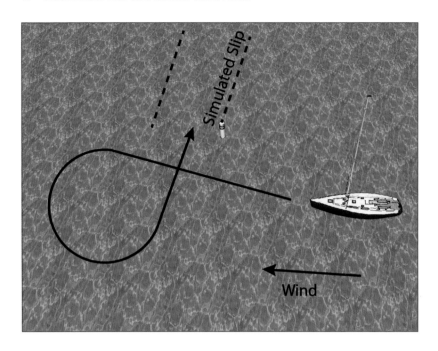

Chapter 3
Prop Walk

Understanding and utilizing propeller walk (or "prop walk") is an integral part of learning how to reverse a sailboat, so we'll go into an in-depth discussion of prop walk here

> **Exercise 7:** With the boat facing downwind and idling at 1000 rpm, put the boat into reverse at 2000 rpm and try to hold a steady course.
>
> **What you learned:** The stern of the boat wants to go to the port (in most boats).

The movement of the stern of the boat to port can be frustrating, but you can learn to use it to your advantage. First, let's understand why the stern goes to port. Imagine you're walking up a spiral staircase. Each step is the same height and requires the same amount of energy to go up to the next step.

Now imagine the spiral staircase was tilted over 20 degrees. You'd find that as you went around the stairs they would be steeper on one side and flatter on the other. Or the steeper side would cut through more vertical space than the flatter side.

As we look at a propeller and the water flowing through it, the arc that the tips of the propeller follow relative to the moving water pushed by the propeller is a spiral shape, much like a spiral staircase.

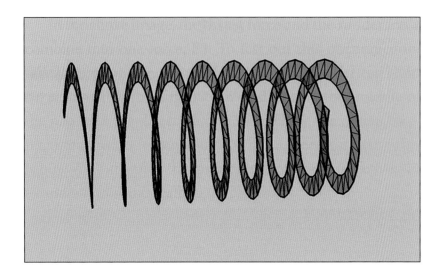

Another way to see it is to observe the sweep of each blade as it passes through the water.

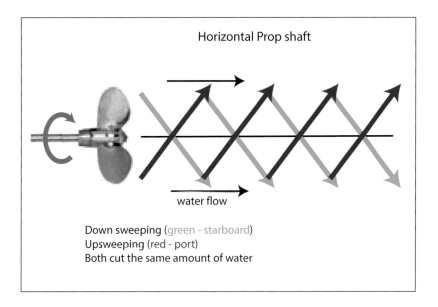

Now, if we tilt the shaft of the propeller down, the spiral also tilts down.

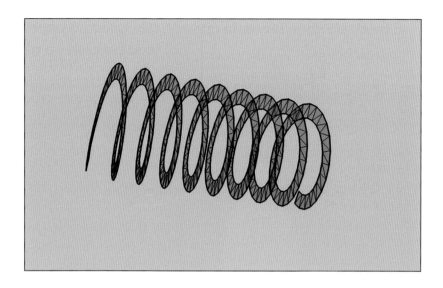

But we have to put a few prefaces on this: there must be no boat hull above to affect the initial flow of water; the water must be deep; and the propeller cannot be moving horizontally through the water—that's a lot of prefaces and not reality. But here is what that would look like anyway.

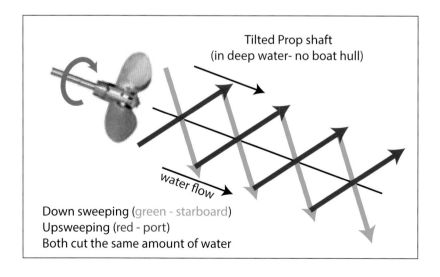

Tilted Prop shaft
(in deep water- no boat hull)

water flow

Down sweeping (green - starboard)
Upsweeping (red - port)
Both cut the same amount of water

Now put the propeller in close to the hull of the boat where the water tends to move horizontally. This is represented by the imaginary sweep lines. Here you can see that the upswinging reversing blade (in green – starboard) cuts more of the flowing water, similar to the tilting staircase example above.

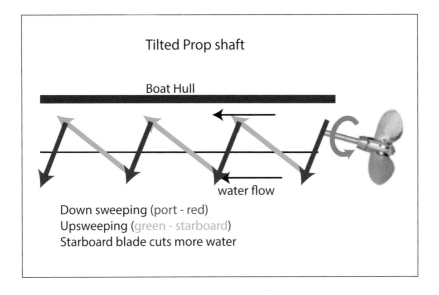

In much the same way as the tilting staircase, the down sweeping blade cuts through less flowing water than the upsweeping blade. This creates more force on the upswinging side of the propeller than the downswinging side, and thus a torque is produced on the prop shaft.

This results in the following forces and a resultant clockwise torque on the boat.

In a similar fashion, imagine yourself treading water in a swimming pool and your right arm swings in big circles while your left swings in smaller circles. Your body would move backwards, but the action would also turn your face to the right and consequently your back to the left. The boat turns in exactly the same way.

In forward gear the exact same phenomenon occurs, just in the opposite direction. However, we notice it much less because the water from the propeller is being pushed over the rudder, which creates far greater forces and thus counteracts any tilt-induced torque.

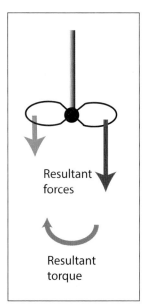

Resultant forces

Resultant torque

So in summary, a boat that has a counter-rotating shaft, when in reverse, yaws clockwise (stern to the left) because the shaft is tilting downwards. Factors to reduce the effect include having a smaller diameter propeller or reducing the pitch (twist) of the blade or lengthening the shaft so that the water flow is further from the boat, which would tend to allow the water flow to be more in line with the shaft. The effect is also reduced by a slower turning propeller, that is, less engine rpm.

An alternative way of mounting the propeller is called a "saildrive," and these are widely accepted in Europe. Saildrive systems have a horizontally mounted propeller shaft and therefore they do not create prop walk.

But there is no need to go to the expense of converting your boat to a saildrive unit if you are experiencing frustration with prop walk. Because now that you understand the theory, (more than 90% of sailors do) all you have to do is practice the exercises a few times and you'll have it licked.

A Saildrive Unit

Turning Your Boat in a Tight Marina

You can use prop walk to turn your boat in a tight marina by applying forward and reverse gears at appropriate times, leaving the rudder locked to starboard.

Watch this animation.

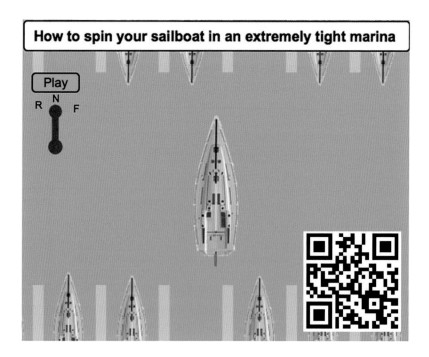

Exercise 8: Use prop walk to turn the boat at a minimum radius. Pretend you are in an extremely tight marina. You have little ability to go forward or backwards. This exercise will show you how you can actually do a donut, and it will allow you to round out of the circle in any direction desired.

With the boat facing upwind and close to a stop, put the wheel hard over to starboard and lock off the wheel. Rev the engine in forward gear to 2500 rpm for 2 seconds only.

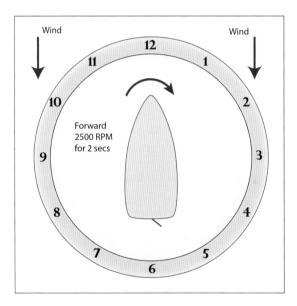

As the boat comes around so that the wind is abeam to port, put the engine into reverse at 2300 rpm; the back of the boat will move to port and thus continue your turn. Note that in reverse you'll find 2500 rpm probably causes a lot of vibration and is not too efficient. Better to use 2300 rpm.

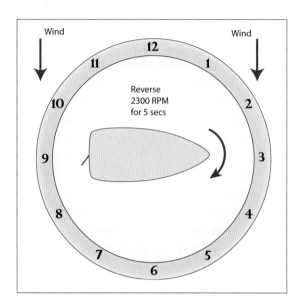

Remember that the wheel stays hard over to starboard. You might think that the wheel needs to go the other way because you are in reverse, but since the boat is still slightly moving forward, water is still flowing forward over the rudder even though the engine is in reverse. And even when the boat comes to a standstill, having the rudder hard over to starboard will not affect the prop walk tendency to port.

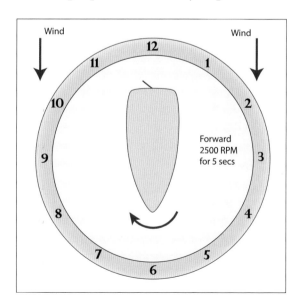

Now, as the stern of the boat goes through the wind, pump the engine back into forward to 2500 rpm. Rev the engine just long enough to prevent any forward motion but long enough to get the boat turning up through the wind to at least the 10 o'clock position so that the turning momentum will carry your bow through the wind without gaining any appreciable forward momentum.

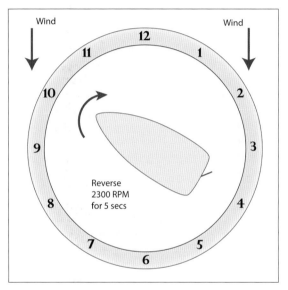

As the bow of the boat is approaching the wind, put the engine back into reverse at 2300 rpm and watch again as the stern moves to port. You can continue this exercise until you feel comfortable. As you become expert at this, gauge the amount of time in forward and reverse to reduce your turning circle diameter.

What you learned: The boat never gains any real forward momentum, and therefore the turning circle can be very tight. However, you are able to maintain very good control over the direction and position of the boat even with high winds.

Note

The boat has its greatest turning ability into the wind when the engine is in forward and the prop is pushing water over the rudder. The wind always wants to push the front of the boat downwind, so use reverse when the wind will work in conjunction—that is, when you want the front of the boat to go downwind during that part of the donut. In high winds, you need to pay particular attention to having the engining in forward gear between 6 o'clock and 10 o'clock. This is so that you can drive the front of the boat upwind. The port prop walk will not be enough to overcome the force of the wind wanting to push the bow downwind. In low winds, you'll not need to concern yourself with this effect.

Note

You can only do this when turning to starboard because the prop walk moves the stern to the port. Just turn the wheel to starboard and lock it off.

In performing the previous exercise (really performing—not just reading), you'll gain a great appreciation for how to use prop walk to your advantage. Now let's move on to reversing exercises.

Chapter 4
Maneuvering in Reverse

Reversing a boat has become quite a favorite of mine and is fun to teach. Please don't just give these exercises lip service. Actually get out and do them and—who cares if others are watching—you'll be able to out-back and out-maneuver them any time after this. It's a practiced skill that you'll be glad you did next time you're in a tight marina in some exotic place with 20 knots of wind on the side and everyone is watching you. The question is, will they be nervous or impressed? It's up to you.

This exercise should take about 30 minutes and is really fun to do. Please actually do it rather than just read it. You'll learn so much and be incredibly confident afterwards. It's more effective to do this on a windy day. Pick a buoy (or ideally 2) that are about 5 boat lengths apart and are out away from the marina. And, of course, during the exercises keep a good watch out for traffic.

Exercise 9: With the boat stopped and pointing downwind, first put the wheel hard over and then rev the engine in reverse to 2300 rpm for about 2 seconds.

What you learned: The boat is not nearly as responsive as the same exercise in forward. In fact, it is doubtful that anything actually happened. Except a bit of prop walk.

Note

The rudder only responds to act on the boat when water is flowing over it. When in reverse, the propeller does not help to push water over the rudder, and thus control of the boat is only achieved by reverse motion of the boat.

Propeller has no effect
on rudder in reverse

Note

Whenever the boat is reversing, *do not* take your hands off the wheel or allow it to spin. The fulcrum of the rudder is at the front. Water moving over the rudder will cause the rudder to slam sideways and potentially break the wheel controls. *Always* keep a hand tightly on the wheel. This effect is like trying to hold a sheet of plywood on the downwind edge against the wind without it flipping around on you—almost impossible. When it flips, it's going to hurt. Same as the wheel: when the back-flowing water pushes against the rudder it can whip the rudder over, spin the wheel very fast, and slam the workings for the wheel-to-rudder connections very hard and very likely cause damage. Backing in a marina with high winds is the last place you want the rudder connection to come off. Scared? Don't be. Just don't let go of the wheel when backing.

Note

Whenever in reverse, only put the wheel a maximum of 80 percent of the way hard over. If it is all the way over, the rudder acts more like a vertical bulldozer blade and reduces the turning effectiveness.

Note

When shifting from forward into reverse and vice versa, *always* stop in neutral for 1 to 2 seconds before shifting gears. Drifting in a marina under high winds and a sheared propeller shaft key is not something you want to experience. Scared? Don't be. Just don't shift the gear lever fast.

Exercise 10: With the boat pointed at about 30 degrees off the wind and idling forward at about 1000 rpm, put the engine into reverse while attempting to hold the boat straight and then begin to back up.

What you learned: On a windy day this is near impossible. The wind will take over and push the bow downwind as soon as the boat stops, and thus water stops flowing over the rudder. Regaining control and trying to get the boat to begin backing up while staying on course is difficult and will use up a lot of space, which is at a premium in a marina. So instead always start your backing with the wind to your stern, even if that has you initially pointing in the wrong direction.

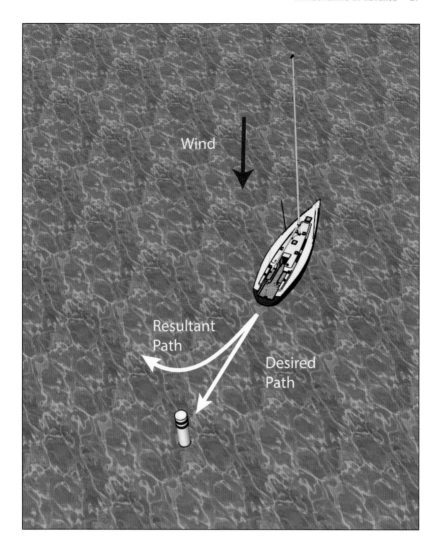

Even if you try it the other way to counteract the prop walk, in high enough winds your bow will still be blown downwind.

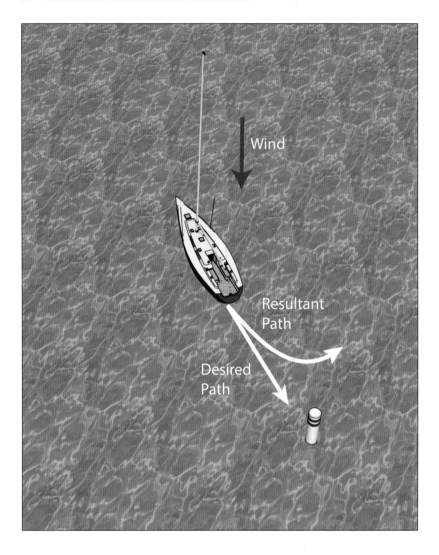

Exercise 11: With the boat stopped and positioned stern to wind—just hang out for a sec and observe the boat's behavior. Then move into forward gear at about 1000 rpm and slowly move forward. Now put the engine in reverse at 2000 rpm. Watch the boat come to a stop and begin backing up.

What you learned: You'll first notice that sitting there with your stern to the wind is a stable position for the boat to be in; that is, the wind really does nothing to the boat and you can hang out like this for a while—especially in a marina when you are waiting for other boats to clear out or deciding which slip to go into. Besides a bit of prop walk, once you start going backwards the boat will hold course and will back straight without all the space used up in the exercise above. Therefore, whenever possible, always begin backing with the stern of the boat facing upwind. Let's repeat that and put it in bold: **whenever possible, always begin backing with the stern of the boat facing upwind.**

Note

There will be some effect from the prop walk which will turn the stern of the boat to port. So learn to anticipate prop walk; that is, you know the boat is going to pull stern to port, so angle your boat as such before you start to reverse.

Note

Simple rule of thumb for steering a boat backwards: if you want the back of the boat to go one way, then turn the wheel that way. Actually, this is the same for going forwards: if you want the front of a boat to go right, then turn to the right. This is why you see some people turn around and get in front of the wheel when going backwards because it is the same as going forwards. As you get used to backing like this, and especially by practicing doing figure 8's around buoys, you'll no longer need to step around the wheel.

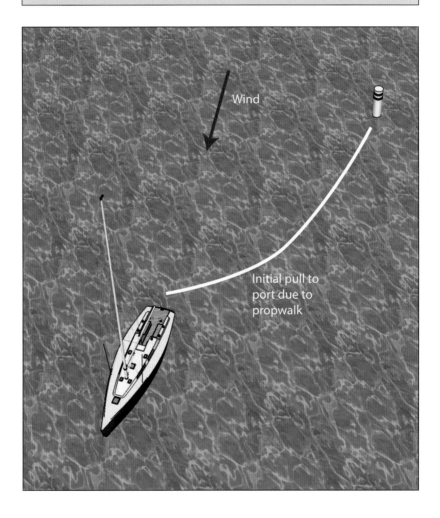

Exercise 12: With the boat facing downwind and the helm centered, put the engine in reverse at about 1500 rpm and begin to back up. You'll notice some prop walk, but continue to move backwards. Turn the wheel to starboard a half turn and hold for 5 seconds. Now turn the wheel back to center and over to port for 5 seconds. Now repeat the exercise at 800 rpm and 2500 rpm.

What you learned: The boat walks to port initially, but after the boat begins to move, the flow of water over the rudder as the boat gains speed overcomes the prop walk and you can turn the boat in any direction. With different rpm you'll notice different turn-rate performance, especially in high-wind conditions. In fact, at 800 rpm you may not even be able to get the boat moving in reverse at all. However, at 2500 rpm you may experience too much initial prop walk, but once the boat is moving you have plenty of speed to overcome prop walk and wind effects. What you may find is that you can start the boat moving in reverse at a lower rpm to minimize prop walk (then raise the engine rpm once the rudder water flow takes effect) and to have good steerage control. Don't be timid with your engine rpm. The faster water is flowing over the rudder, the better control you have of the boat. Gain some experience using this exercise to get a feel for maneuverability versus engine rpm.

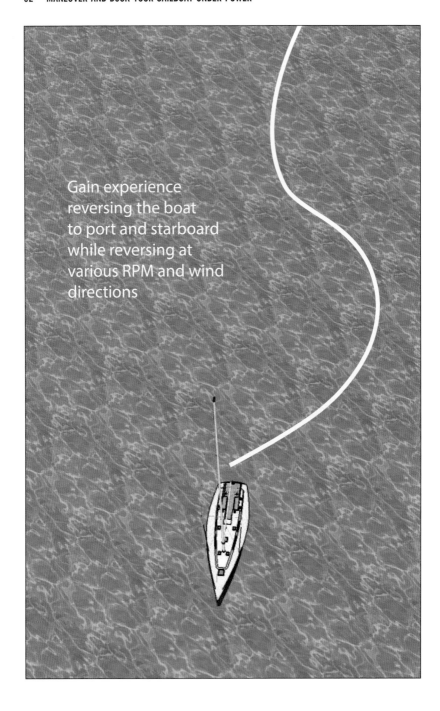

Gain experience
reversing the boat
to port and starboard
while reversing at
various RPM and wind
directions

Exercise 13: While backing up into the wind at 2000 rpm, turn the wheel to port so that it is 80 percent of the way hard over. Allow the boat to do a complete circle.

What you learned: You'll notice that the boat begins to turn quite easily and the radius of turn is again surprisingly tight.

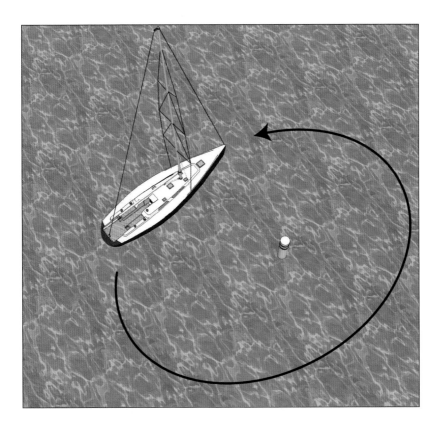

And you can even do it in the opposite direction. Although you'll deal with a little bit of prop walk at the start, once underway you'll be turning the boat however you want.

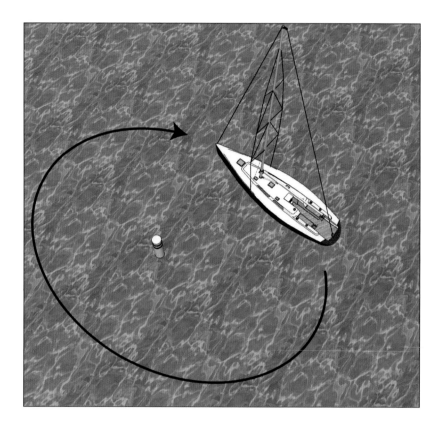

Exercise 14: Try to do the same backing maneuver at 800 rpm.

What you learned: You notice that on a windy day you'll be unable to achieve a complete circle. Again, the flow of water over the rudder is the determining factor and is only gained in reverse by boat speed. In close quarters, trying to maneuver the boat without water flowing over the rudder will cause damage to something or somebody. Get that water flowing. Don't be afraid to use rpm.

Exercise 15: Pick a buoy and do 5 donuts in reverse around the buoy at 2000 rpm. Adjust the wheel position so as not to hit the buoy but keep it as close to 80 percent hard over as possible. Then straighten out the wheel and back up straight with the wind abeam.

What you learned: It is relatively easy to back the boat around like this, and even with the wind abeam you can hold a straight course.

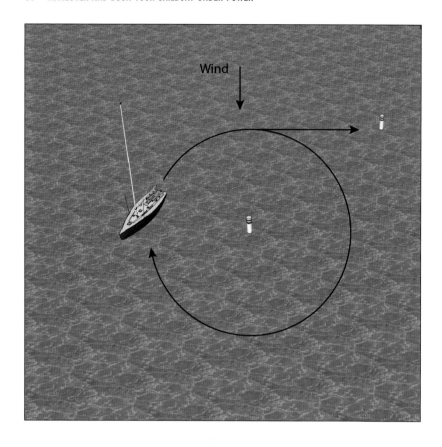

Exercise 16: Do figure 8's around 2 buoys leaving the engine at 2000 rpm. Use imaginary buoys if none are present. The figure 8 should be about 5 boat lengths.

What you learned: You should begin to gain confidence in how the boat maneuvers under power going backwards.

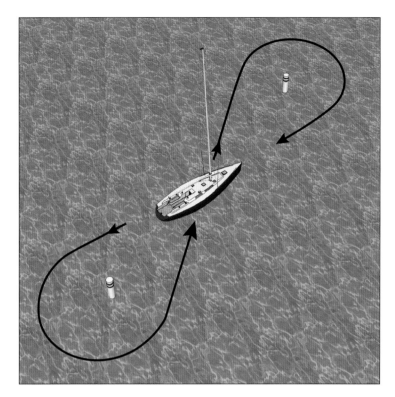

Now it's time to start to learn backing into a slip. But we'll first start it outside the marina and next to a buoy. Use the buoy as a reference and your imagination to create the docking scenarios below.

Exercise 17: Pretend you're backing up to a dock. With your boat positioned downwind from a buoy, back up to the buoy and stop the boat so that the buoy is positioned 4 feet off the back of the boat. Use forward gear as you get close to the buoy.

What you learned: The boat stops extremely fast, in fact, if you use too much forward you'll find yourself driving back downwind and away from the "dock" that you're supposed to be tying off to. You'll probably notice that just a spurt of power in forward will do the trick to stop the boat in position. Repeat the exercise so that you can stop the boat effectively in the correct position.

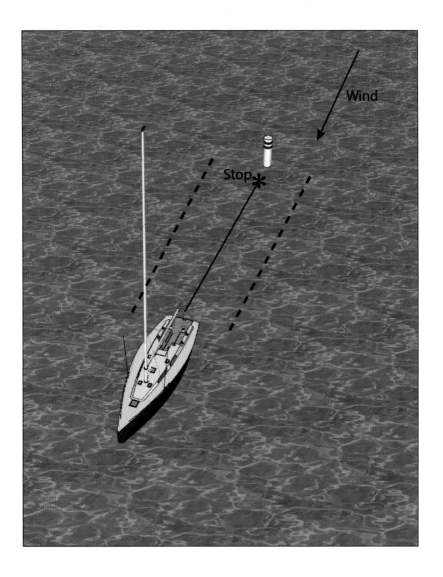

Exercise 18: Repeat the exercise from upwind and crosswind.

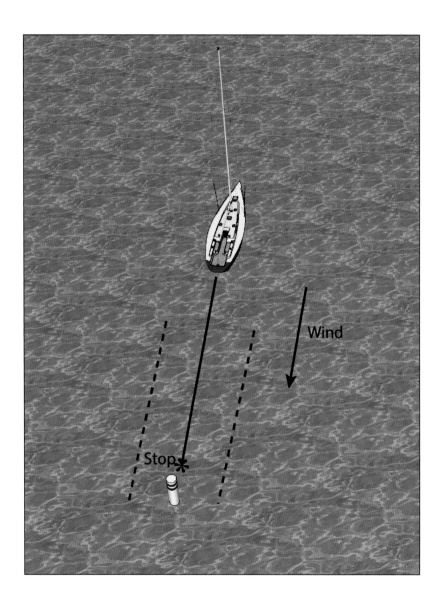

What you learned: Here is a crucial learning point. If you stopped too early and try to start going backwards again, you're going to be forced off-course by prop walk and the wind on your bow at the exact point where it is imperative to keep straight. So it's important to not stop too early as you will have absolutely no control. What this means is that you must practice, practice, practice backing downwind and stopping at the right point every time. Get used to how much power it takes to stop the boat, and discovering exactly when you should apply that power. The only way out of this situation is to apply forward power and start the whole procedure again 50 yards out.

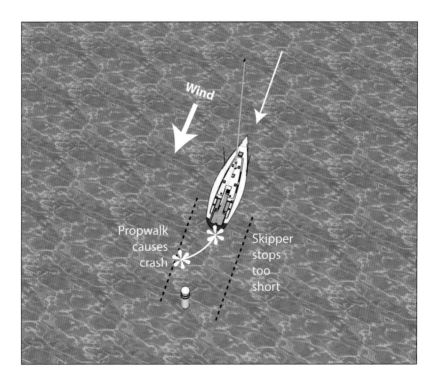

Exercise 19: Assume you wanted to back into a downwind-facing slip. Pretend the buoy is the pylon next to your slip. Start with the boat facing downwind, begin backing and do a U-turn and back the boat into the slip.

What you learned: This is a simple maneuver that could have been trouble if you did not start facing downwind; that is, we're teaching you to always start with your stern to the wind.

Note

Simple rule of thumb for steering a boat backwards: If you want the back of the boat to go one way, then turn the wheel that way. Actually, this is the same for going forwards—if you want the front of a boat to go right, then turn to the right. This is why you see some people turn around and get in front of the wheel when going backwards because it is the same as going forwards. As you get used to backing like this (and especially practicing doing figure 8's around buoys), you'll no longer need to step around the wheel.

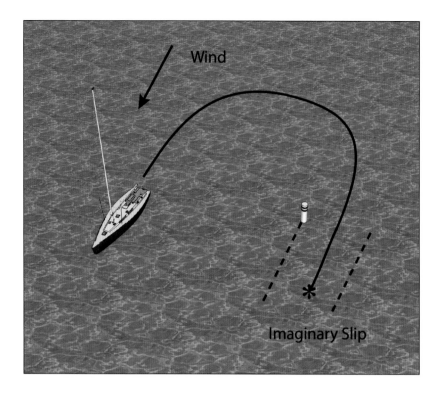

Summary: So Now You Get It, Right?

- Always begin with your stern to the wind, then maneuver your boat backwards into the position you want by doing right-angle turns, U-turns, or backing straight in.
- Once the water is flowing over the rudder, you can maneuver the boat however you want.
- Just don't stop the boat unless you're either tied off or your stern is to the wind.
- Use enough speed to create rudder flow in order to overcome the wind.
- Don't be afraid to use plenty of power.
- Start with low revs to reduce prop walk, then increase as the boat begins to move.

- Anticipate prop walk.
- If you have to stop and wait for traffic, then do it with your stern to the wind.
- And if you can only remember one thing from this entire course—it is stern to the wind.

Chapter 5

Sideways Movement and Spinning

Fighter pilots are familiar with the term *VIF-ing*. VIF stands for "vectoring in flight." It means that you can move your plane sideways, up or down while in flight. The British-designed Harrier fighter with its vertical takeoff capability has the greatest ability for VIF-ing because of its control thrusters.

Likewise, you can make your sailboat go sideways—at least the stern. Or in the case of an installed bow thruster, the whole boat can maneuver sideways. And in many cases this is just what the doctor ordered to get you into the dock or away from an obstacle.

You can typically easily tell what position your rudder is in by observing your autopilot meter—if installed.

This indicates that the rudder is 20 degrees to starboard and thus

your wheel is also over to starboard. If you engage forward, which way will your stern move?

Exercise 20: With your stern to the wind, or on a calm day and the boat is at a standstill next to a buoy, put the wheel hard over to port and engage forward for 1 second. Repeat the exercise with the wheel to starboard.

What you learned: The stern of the boat moved to port if the wheel was turned to starboard, and to starboard if the wheel was turned to port.

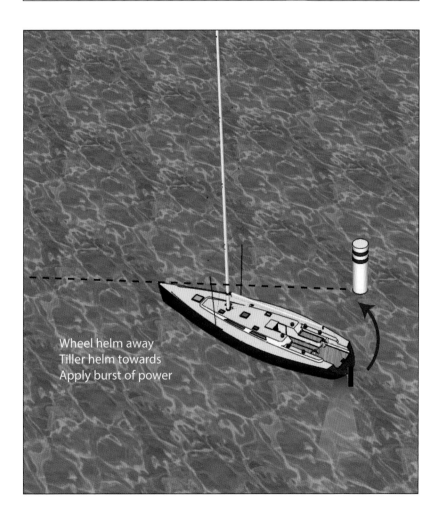

Wheel helm away
Tiller helm towards
Apply burst of power

Effectively Using a Bow Thruster

Exercise 21: With your stern to the wind, or on a calm day and the boat is at a standstill next to a buoy, engage the bow thruster for 1 second to starboard.

What you learned: The bow of the boat moved to starboard while the stern remained still or perhaps moved slightly to port. This is because the boat will tend to pivot about a point slightly rear of the keel (due to the drag of the rudder as well).

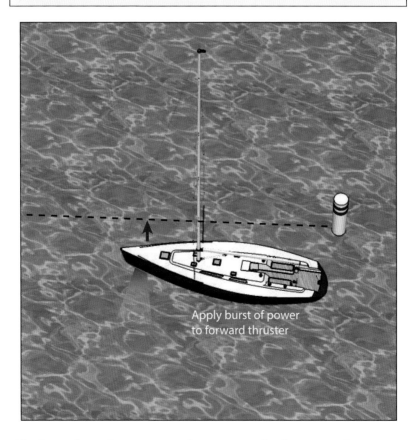

Apply burst of power
to forward thruster

Ah, but what about using the two methods in combination?

Exercise 22: With your stern to the wind, or on a calm day and the boat is at a standstill next to a buoy, put the wheel hard over to port and engage forward for 1 second and engage the bow thruster to starboard.

What you learned: The whole boat moved laterally (VIF-ed) to starboard.

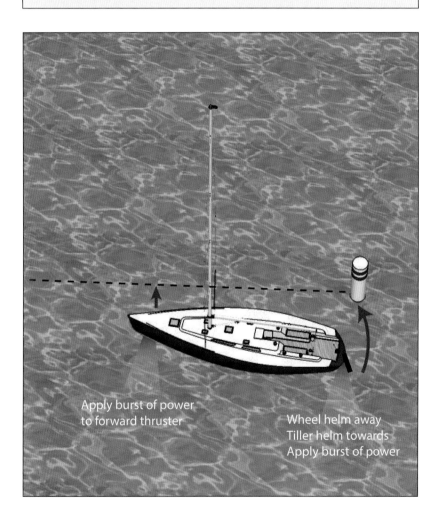

Apply burst of power
to forward thruster

Wheel helm away
Tiller helm towards
Apply burst of power

Exercise 23: Play with the bow thruster and get a feel for the bow sideways movement versus the pivoting point about which the boat moves. Experiment with the port thruster and reverse to use prop walk to vector the boat to port. Spin the boat using starboard thruster and wheel to starboard. Lock the wheel to starboard and use the port thruster and a combination of forward and reverse gear to prevent any appreciable forward momentum gain to move the boat continuously to port. Try the same to move the boat laterally to starboard; while not as effective as to port due to prop walk, you can still do it.

What you learned: You can spin the boat on its own pivot point. You can move the boat sideways. Now also try these exercises in high wind conditions at various angles to the wind.

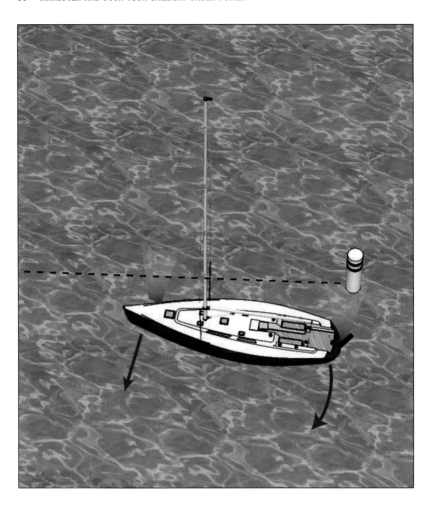

Chapter 6
Using Spring Lines

Spring lines are incredibly useful in getting you into and out of a slip, onto and off the Tee-head, or making you look like an expert in a Mediterranean mooring situation.

The concept is pretty simple: you're using the force imparted from a line to the dock against the forces from the propeller to position and turn your boat however you want.

The action of using a line to help maneuver the boat is called "springing on" or "springing off"—thus the lines used are called "spring lines." But they are usually just plain old dock lines.

Essentially, you need to know how to apply and control the force in every scenario. Half the time, the wind and current will work for you or are of little effect so you don't need a spring line. But the other half of the time, if you don't spring on or off (or in or out), you'll be putting your name on the amateur sailor's list.

You can always tell if you're doing it right in a busy marina. If people are getting up and putting fenders out and pointing and telling you what to do, they have already labeled you as an amateur. If they keep sipping their gin and tonics, you're looking good.

Force Alignment and Moment Balance

There is a really cool universal law out there that states: "For every force there must be an equal and opposite force." When you are docking, if your boat pulls on a line attached to the dock, the line pulls back on your boat. If the forces are aligned, nothing really happens.

When the forces are not aligned, the forces work on their own volition to try to align themselves through a phenomenon called torque—also known as "moment." (Not a moment in time, but rather a force applied at a distance.) The greater the force or distance, the greater the moment. Think of it as a turning force. It is this concept of moment that you must fully understand. So the second part to the universal equation above is that, "For equilibrium (no spin-

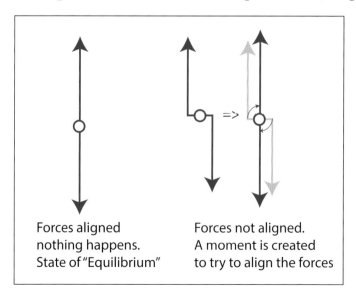

Forces aligned
nothing happens.
State of "Equilibrium"

Forces not aligned.
A moment is created
to try to align the forces

ning) to occur, for every moment there must be an equal and opposite moment." Don't worry, it is all easy and the exercises will allow you to gain an excellent feel for the dynamics (forces and moments).

The image on the previous page shows the forces aligning.

To make things easier, the universe decided that multiple forces applied at the same place are additive. And forces applied at distances can be represented by a turning force in between them.

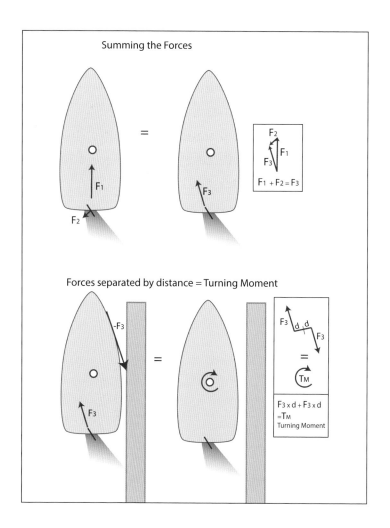

In the above image, the thrust force and the rudder force combine into one force, F3. To test out this phenomenon, take your phone and place it on a desk. Hold the top right corner down with a finger then push the bottom middle of the phone in the direction of F3. You'll see the phone turn. It's kinda obvious when you do this but, needless to say, this is how you can apply this process to your boat to get you in to and out of some really tight places.

The image below shows what happens to a boat when tied to the dock at a sternside cleat and propeller thrust is engaged. All the forces align and moments balance to move the boat to an equilibrium position.

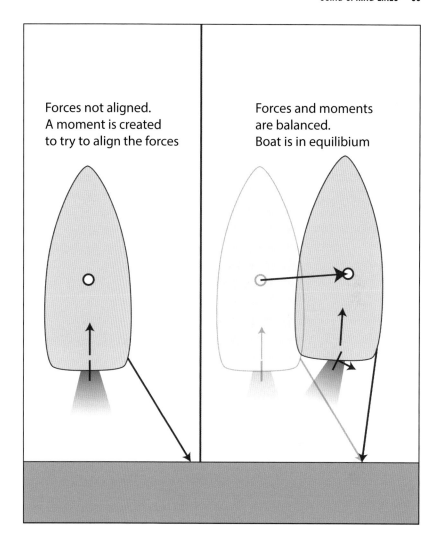

Forces not aligned.
A moment is created
to try to align the forces

Forces and moments
are balanced.
Boat is in equilibium

Notice the rudder is slightly turned. The rudder is apply-ing an additional balancing force to stabilize the boat.

Rudder Force

The rudder can be a big help because it can change the direction of the thrust force.

Simply by turning the rudder, you can change the entire dynamics of the force and moment balancing equations.

Thus, you can turn the boat in a desired direction and also gain advantage over the wind and current. For example, you can prevent your bow from being blown downwind. When springing, you can make your bow actually turn upwind.

In the image below, the rudder is turned and the stern of the boat feels forward and sideways forces aft, which acts to turn the boat.

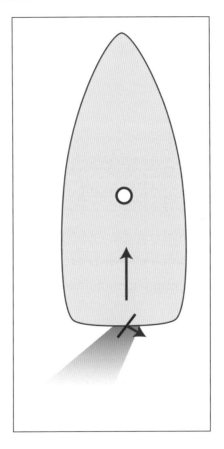

Below, if the boat is tied to the dock, the forward thrust is counterbalanced by the spring line but the force on the rudder changes how the boat sits. Thus, if the rudder angle is increased the boat changes position.

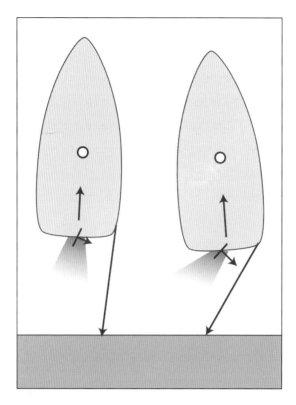

In a side wind, working the rudder is particularly useful to "spring" your boat to windward or let it drift down to leeward. You are using your engine speed and rudder to achieve equilibrium.

Spring Line Exercise 1

In a crosswind across a Tee-head dock, tie your windward stern cleat to the Tee-head with at least 10 feet (3 meters) of space from your stern to the dock. Now engage forward gear and have a play once the spring line is taut. Turn the wheel to port and starboard. Gain an appreciation for how your boat reacts. Try higher and lower throttle settings. Note that when you turn the wheel to leeward the boat climbs to windward.

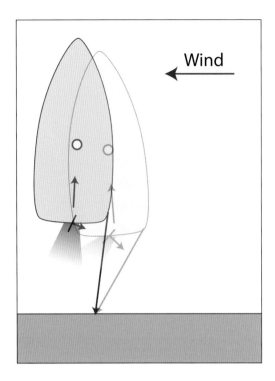

Spring Line Exercise 2

With the same setup as above, slowly turn the wheel to windward and slowly bring the bow of the boat all the way to the dock. Congratulations—you just springed your boat into the dock by turning your bow into the wind. Your boat's "bum" will be hanging out a bit because of the thrust vector on the rudder, but at least you are at the dock now. Lock the wheel and leave the thrust engaged. Now leave the helm and go forward to the bow, taking a dock line with you. Cleat the bow to the dock at a position about amidships on the dock. Return to the helm and slowly turn the wheel the other way—away from the dock. Watch the stern suck right into the dock. Now tighten up the stern line. Take a break in amazement at how easy that was and that you did it all by your lonesome self.

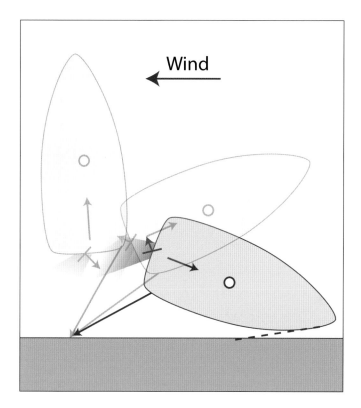

You can now see that by thinking about the forces and using the rudder you can master all kinds of docking scenarios with all kinds of current and wind conditions. Additionally, you can place the spring lines, forward, amidships or aft. By placing spring lines amidships or forward at the bow, you are increasing the distance between the thrust/rudder force and the spring line force. Since the magnitude of the turning moment is proportional to the distance between the forces, you are able to use this to design your entire maneuver.

Designing the Maneuver

Like a work of fine engineering, a spring maneuver requires a design. The key is to plan the maneuver by considering the wind, current, and other obstacles, then design the placement and directions of the forces and moments.

The decisions are:

1. What to do with the rudder?
2. Forward or reverse gear?
3. Where to place the spring line: aft, amidships, or forward?

Take, for example, the following situation: You have a very tight marina and a strong wind that will prevent you from simply turning out of the slip. Which spring line would you use: 1, 2, or 3?

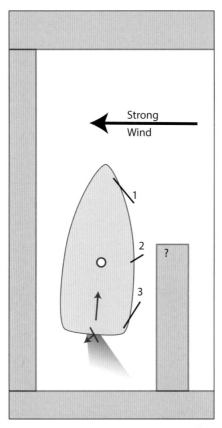

Using an amidships spring line is going to be your best solution. It will keep your boat tight in the turn around the end of the walkway finger and provide enough distance (X) between the rudder force and the spring line force to create an effective turning moment.

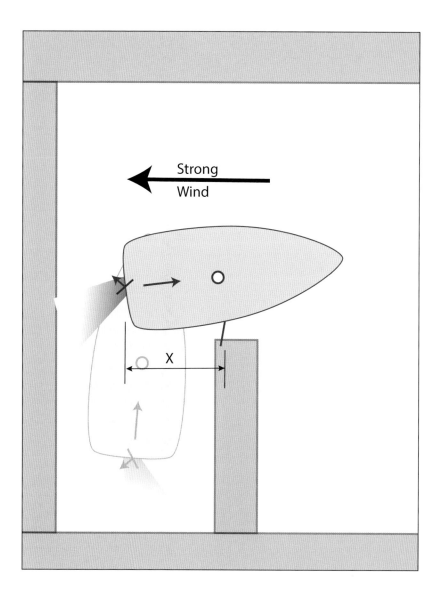

It is obvious even from looking at the image below that putting a spring line aft is not going to work because distance X is too small and no appreciable turning moment is created. Additionally, a forward spring line would not work so well because it would require the aft to swing into the port dock wall.

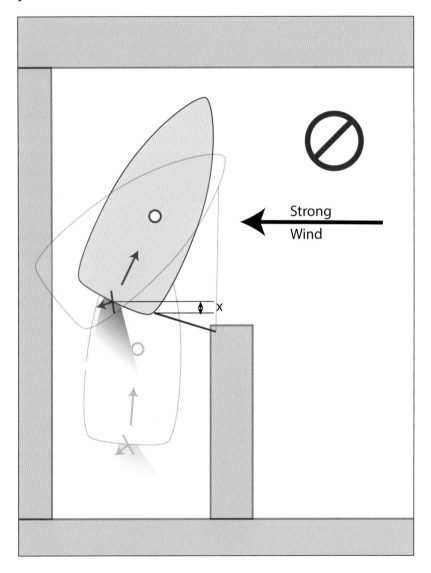

Strong Wind

Spring Line Exercise 3

Try the above springing out of the slip maneuver on a day with crosswind.

When designing a spring maneuver, you should look at how the wind or current will affect your boat. For example, you would *not* do this maneuver to leave the dock if the wind or current were high.

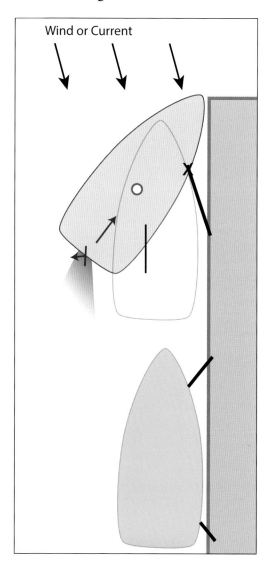

Despite good force and moment thoughts, the overall design is poor. The wind or current could blow you down into the boat parked behind you.

Instead, you would get out using either one of these maneuvers. In both cases notice the direction of forces and imagine the turning moment created.

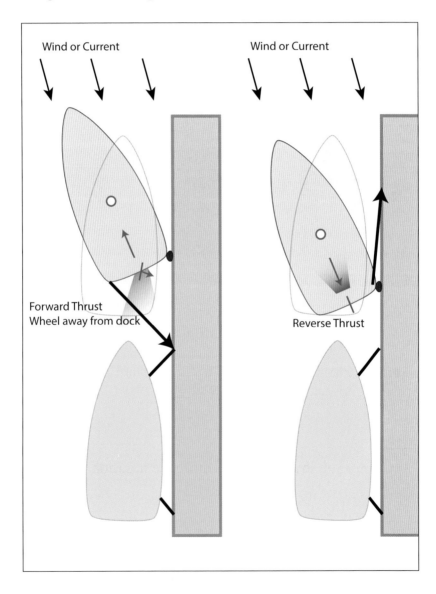

In the reverse thrust example, you'll notice the rudder is not turned. This is because the rudder has little effect on redirecting the water flow when in reverse. Also notice that in both cases a force component is toward the dock—and thus a fender between the dock and the boat is a good idea.

Here are two other effective springing off and out examples, and another that will not work.

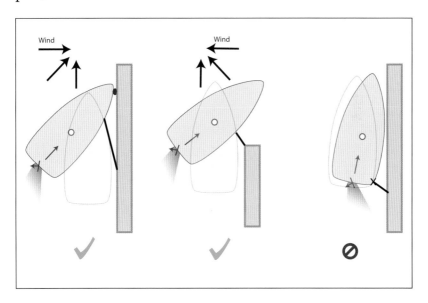

Springing On and In

Coming into a slip is usually not a problem and does not require a spring because you merely drive the boat in either forward or reverse. Once you are in, you can sort out the details.

Coming up to a Tee-head is more the situation where you need to spring on. The need for accuracy in your maneuver is heightened when the space is tight. Here is an animation of a boat doing this.

And here are the forces and moment diagrams.

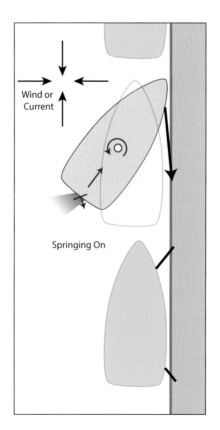

After you make your plan, ensure dock lines are made ready and (very important) that the crew are told exactly which direction to cleat the boat when they get off. In high winds things can go south very quickly.

Plan to get the bow of the boat sprung to the dock, and then to spring in.

If you're going it alone, there is usually quicker access to the dock from the cockpit. Below the skipper steps off, taking the amidships spring line to the dock, then powers the boat around using the spring line. The spring line at amidships provides extra distance between the forces and, thus, extra turning moment.

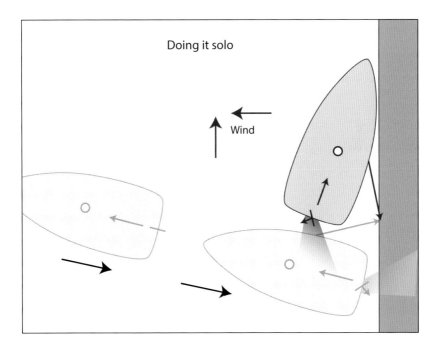

Doing it solo

Wind

Chapter 7
Leaving the Dock

OK, now that we're experts at maneuvering the boat under power, we'll review the maneuvering in and out of a marina using the instructions presented in the NauticEd Skipper Course. This shows the various maneuvering one should do based on wind conditions and slip position.

Prior to Push Off:

1. Start engine and ensure it is adequately warmed up.
2. Ensure everything is stowed.
3. No dock lines are in the water to tangle the prop.
4. Center the wheel.
5. Guests who do not have assigned jobs should be seated.
6. Give clear instructions to each crew member on their coming tasks.
7. Assess the wind and current direction at the slip so you can be prepared to keep control of the vessel under the prevailing conditions.

The following diagrams show you how to use wind and current to your advantage.

END TIES

Wind pushing you away from the dock

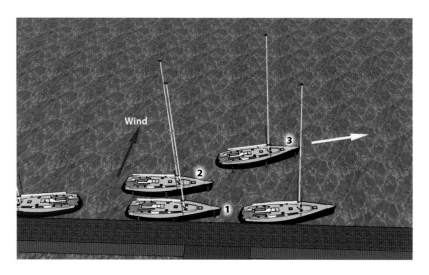

This is the simplest scenario:

1. Once you are confident of your plan, release and stow dock lines, then allow the wind to push the boat clear of other obstacles.
2. Engage the gear lever.
3. Use enough power to overcome the effects from the wind. Head out to enjoy the day.

Wind coming from behind

This is a little more tricky. If you try to go out forwards, the wind could potentially push you into other boats. Additionally, as you turn the wheel to head out, the rear

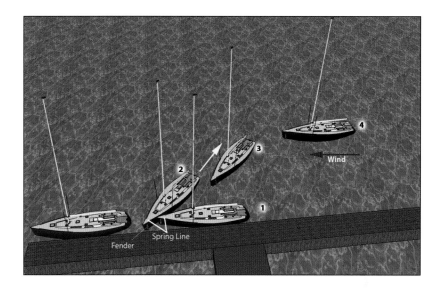

of the boat will swing around towards the dock and other boats. Therefore, it is recommended that you reverse out using a spring line.

Once you are confident of your plan:

1. Appoint a crew member to use a fender at the front of the boat to prevent the boat from touching the dock.

2. Release and stow the dock lines, but leave one spring line from the dock near the center of the boat attached to the front of the boat.

3. The spring line should be arranged so that it is attached to the forward cleat, runs freely around the dock cleat, and returns back to the appointed crew member. In this manner the crew member can release the line and retrieve it by letting it slip around the dock cleat. *Ensure* that there are no knots in the line to get caught on the dock cleat as it runs through.

4. Turn the wheel towards the dock and engage forward gear.

5. This will have the effect of pushing the rear of the boat away from the dock.

Once the boat has turned out from the dock, engage reverse and have your forward crew member release and retrieve the spring line.

Continue backing out to be completely clear before engaging forward gear. Remember, the rear of the boat will swing back towards the dock once you engage forward and turn the wheel to windward, so ensure there is plenty of room.

Wind pushing into the dock and current from behind

You can use exactly the same method as described above.

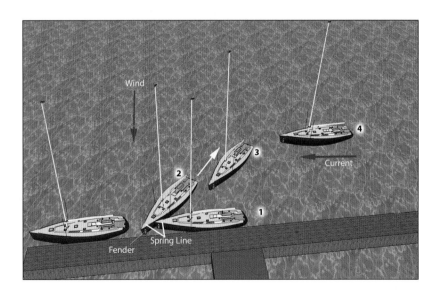

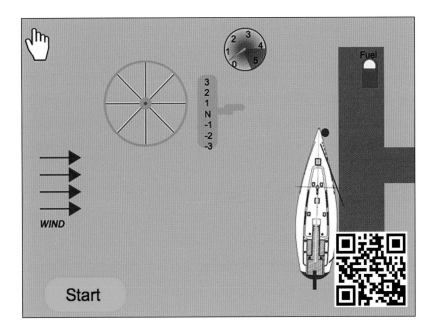

Here is an animation that will help with this. Scan the QR code.

Wind pushing into the dock and current from forward

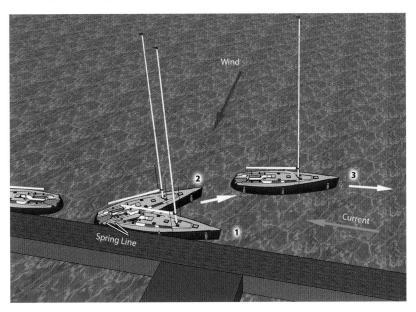

You will have to balance this one a little depending on the strength of the current versus the wind.

If the wind is light you can usually get away with just pushing the front of the boat out. But significant wind may prevent this from happening, and you may need to resort to backing out as in #3 above. Once you are confident of your plan:

1. Appoint a crew member to use a fender at the rear of the boat to prevent the boat from touching the dock.
2. Release and stow the dock lines, but leave one spring line from the dock near the center of the boat attached to the rear of the boat.
3. The spring line should be arranged so that it is attached to the rear cleat, runs freely around the dock cleat, and returns back to the appointed crew member. In this manner the crew member can release the line and retrieve it by letting it slip around the dock cleat. *Ensure* that there are no knots in the line to get caught on the dock cleat as it runs through.
4. Keep the wheel centered and engage reverse gear.
5. This will have the effect of pulling the front of the boat away from the dock.
6. Once the boat has turned out from the dock, engage forward gear and have your crew member release and retrieve the spring line. Remember, the rear of the boat will swing back towards the dock if you turn the wheel. Ensure the boat has swung out enough so that you can motor straight out.
7. Continue maneuvering out until you are completely clear before turning.

SLIPS

Wind coming into the slip channel and your boat is stern to.

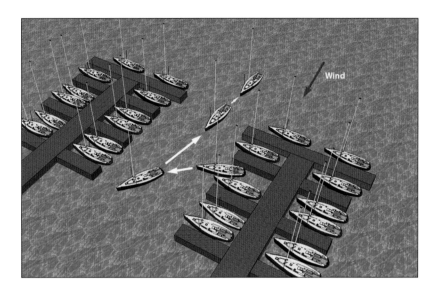

This is best handled by steering out of the slip and then immediately downwind. Back out of the slip channel and well into the main channel before engaging forward.

Wind blowing into the slip channel and your boat is bow to

Simply back out of the slip into the slip channel and then into the main channel. You may need a bow line to the windward dock to prevent the bow blowing downwind as you engage reverse.

Wind blowing out of the slip channel and your boat is bow to

Back out into the wind, then engage forward. Watch for traffic as you enter the main channel.

In higher winds you may need to use some lines to assist. Scan the QR code.

Wind blowing out of the slip channel and your boat is stern to

Simply drive the boat out to the main channel.

Wind blows across the docks and your boat is stern to

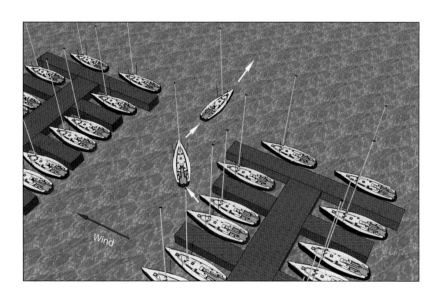

Again, simply drive the boat out to the main channel.

Wind blows across the dock and your boat is bow to

Simply reverse the boat out of the slip, into the slip channel, and then into the main channel. If the wind is light you may elect to turn the boat in the slip channel and come out in forward. However, if the wind is strong it's safer to follow the above diagram.

Other wind/current configurations are solved using variations of the above techniques.

Chapter 8
Returning to the Dock

Time flies when you are sailing, but sadly the moment comes when it is time to return and put your vessel back in its slip. Much of what has to be done to return to the dock is simply the reverse of what was done to get out of the dock and go.

The following are scenarios which will help you in maneuvering a safe and unscratched boat to the dock, or better known as "no damage docking."

END TIES

Wind blowing you off the dock

1. Plan a fairly steep approach so that you are facing more so into the wind. Ensure your speed is just adequate to overcome effects from the wind. Ensure dock lines have been placed on the front and rear of the boat well before you enter the marina. Appoint

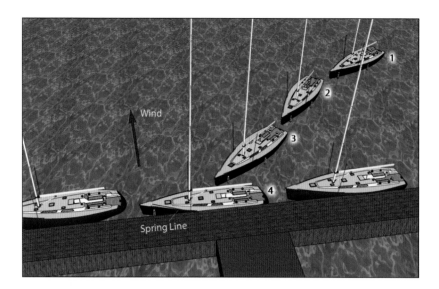

crew members for tying off. Ensure you instruct your crew members not to jump to the dock, but step off once the boat is at the dock.

2. Aim toward the point on the dock where you want the center of the boat to end up. Usually you can put it out of gear about here.

3. Round out just before the dock. Engage reverse.

4. Using a combination of reverse and forward, neatly slide the boat to the dock with zero forward speed. You'll need to have your crew members act smartly to get the boat tied to the dock. In high wind conditions, you should use a spring line from the front of the boat to the center dock cleat. You can then easily turn the wheel away from the dock and engage forward. This will drive the rear of the boat to the dock. Use a fender on the front.

Often times, you'll be coming into a fuel dock or pump out station. View this animation to get into a tight spot.

Wind blowing you into the dock

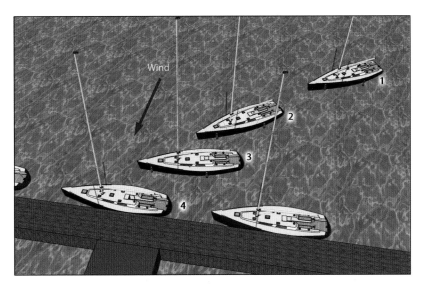

The approach is similar to the above; however, it is a little flatter and your round out is earlier.

Wind from behind

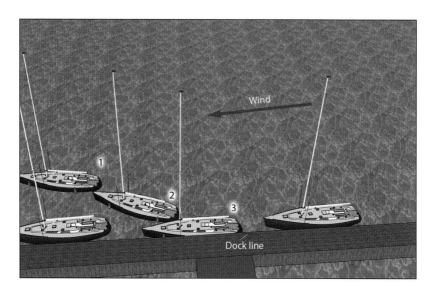

This has potentially dangerous consequences of pushing you into other boats. It is therefore recommended that you back in.

1. Position yourself downwind and facing downwind. Engage reverse.
2. Back the boat toward the point on the dock where you want the center of the boat to end up.
3. Round out and touch forward, if needed, to stop the reverse momentum. Ensure that the first dock line to be attached to the dock is the rear one.

FERRYING

Play the animation below. This shows how to make your boat go sideways to the wind using the wind as your friend and a combination of power and rudder to keep a balance.

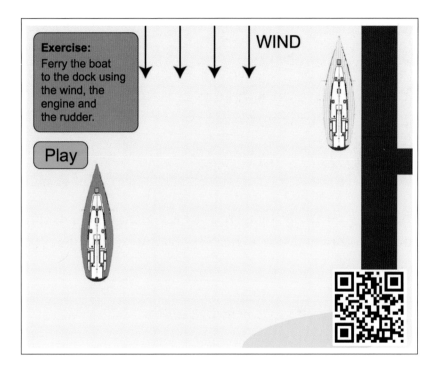

SLIPS

Wind coming into the slip channel and your boat is to be docked stern to

Steer into the slip channel and maneuver past the slip. Engage reverse and back up into the wind, then turn into your dock.

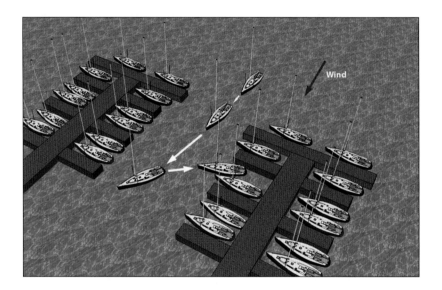

Wind blowing into the slip channel and your boat is to be docked bow to.

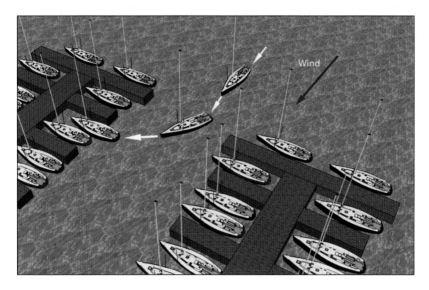

Simply steer the boat into the slip works for light wind; however, the below method is safer for stronger winds.

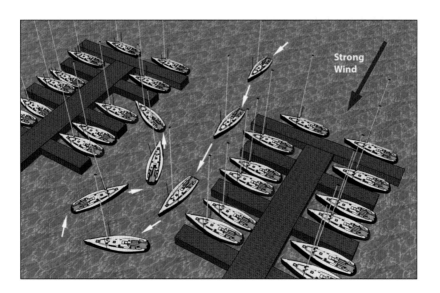

It is preferable to steer the boat up into the wind and into the slip.

Wind blowing out of the slip channel and your boat is to be docked bow to

Simply steer the boat into the slip.

Wind blowing out of the slip channel and your boat is to be docked stern to

Back from the main channel into the slip channel and into your slip.

Wind across the docks and your boat is to be docked stern to

Back from the main channel into the slip channel and into your slip.

Wind blows across the dock and your boat is to be docked bow to

Steer the boat into the slip.

Chapter 9

Mediterranean Mooring

This is where the rubber meets the road—or, in this case, where the gelcoat does *not* touch the big hard concrete wall.

A "Mediterranean Mooring" is so-called because in almost every Mediterranean marina the port authority requires one. You cannot go side-to at the dock.

Once you master this skill, you will find all kinds of scenarios outside of the Mediterranean whereby you will want to and need to perform this maneuver.

Lunch Time Entertainment

On the island of Saint Lucia in Marigot Bay, we wanted to have lunch at JJ's Mangrove Restaurant but all the mooring balls in the bay were occupied. They have a nice dock to pull up to at the back of the bay near the mangroves. We Med-Moored to the dock, all the while everyone in the restaurant was looking on, probably hoping for some disastrous entertainment. We disappointed them by performing the maneuver flawlessly, whereby we received a standing ovation. If you go there, have the jerk chicken. Wow!

In a Mediterranean mooring, you back up to the big hard concrete quay (pronounced *key*) and tie off your stern lines to the quay cleats. And since it is the Med, there is usually a $20 million boat owned by an Arab prince parked on either side of you, so it's a good idea *not* to hit them. Also in the Med, there are certain times of the year when there can be

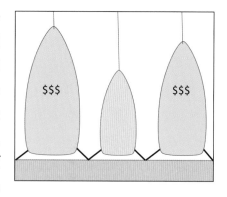

extremely high winds. All this calls for you to be an expert.

But don't stress. With the new maneuvering and backing skills you are learning here and practicing, a Med Mooring will become simple and unintimidating. The first few times it is going to be boat and crew chaos, but not after you become an expert.

What makes a Med Mooring fun is that, after the chaos of getting situated, you get to sit in your cockpit with a good G&T, decompress, and watch the action on the quay—which is usually jammed with bars, restaurants, and passersby. Later, you can stroll along the quay and look into the cockpits of your $20 million neighbors and ponder the life of the rich and famous. It's all good stuff.

Scan the QR code below to see an animation on how to do a Mediterranean Mooring. Click the start button and read along. To continue, click the instructions inside the green box.

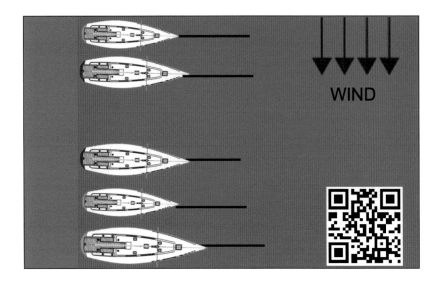

Doing a Med-Mooring requires some very good maneuvering skills, so we highly advise that you practice the teachings here in your home port before you head to the Med.

The key lies in doing it all in one continuous swoop— not stopping short and then trying to restart your aftward motion. If you stop short, your prop walk and the wind will really mess you around. You'll have no water over the rudder and no steerage. Trying to straighten her up and back in again will not work. You'll be better off completely starting again from a distance. If you are well-versed at backing now, this will be easy.

It is important that, when you get ready to stop the boat using forward thrust, you not leave forward thrust on too long—otherwise your boat will start moving forward again away from the quay. You can see how this will quickly turn into a mess: You'll have some crew on the dock, the dock lines will be too short to reach, and your aft crew will be throwing lines into the water while you have the prop churning away. Dock lines will get wrapped around the prop, and you'll be half out of the slip and getting pushed against the next boat by the wind. The engine will be stalled. Everyone will be yelling at you in goodness knows what language. It will be mayhem—all because you left the forward thrust on a little too long. Become a master at stopping the boat dead and putting the throttle into neutral.

Securing the Aft

Once the boat gets close to the dock wall, have some crew ready to step off (no jumping) and receive the stern lines cast to them from crew at the aft. Many times there are willing people strolling the dock who will receive the aft dock lines. Do not expect that those people are experts. Whether it is your crew or the strollers, you must point to exactly which quay cleat to tie to. Pick cleats wide away from your beam.

For now, unless it is a dead-calm day and you performed the maneuver perfectly, don't worry about perfectly tying the aft lines. You can fix and adjust them later. The most important thing is to get the lines tied quickly to the cleat on the quay. This allows you to spring the boat back into position if you need to using thrust over the turned rudder. From above, if you want the boat to go to port, then turn the wheel to starboard and apply forward thrust. Just remember: use opposite wheel direction for movement of your stern.

After you are settled in, undo the knot on the quay cleat and run the line through or around the cleat and back to the boat cleat. This allows for easy release-and-go once you are ready to cast off the next day.

In the image above, the stern line runs from the boat, through a ring on the quay, and back to the boat.

Securing the Bow

There are two types of Med Moorings. The first has a "slime line" attached to the quay wall that leads to a mooring line attached to a sunken concrete block out from the quay. The second requires you to drop the anchor out in the harbor before backing in.

Med Mooring with a slime line.

Once you are cleated to the quay, use a little forward thrust and appropriate rudder angle to hold your boat stable,

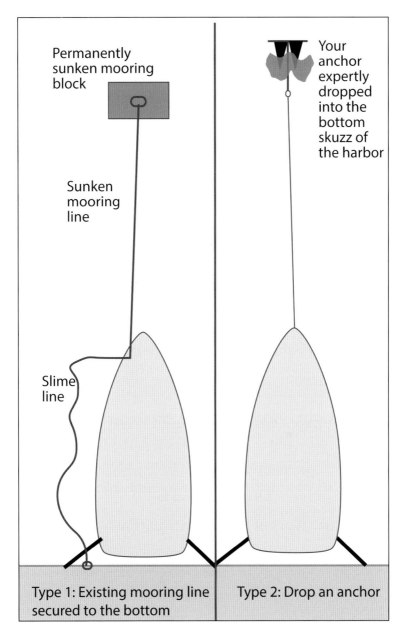

Permanently sunken mooring block

Your anchor expertly dropped into the bottom skuzz of the harbor

Sunken mooring line

Slime line

Type 1: Existing mooring line secured to the bottom

Type 2: Drop an anchor

pointing out and away from the wall. Now a crew member with rubber gloves or a plastic bag covering their hand for slime protection should pick up the slime line from the quay wall and chase it forward to the bow. The slime line is

Mooring line to the sunken mooring block

Slime Line to the quay wall

appropriately named. It is covered completely with viscous and gross slime, since it spends all its life in the water in a harbor. The slime line is attached to the sunken mooring line. At the bow the crew member pulls (and pulls) until the mooring line is found. Now the crew member pulls tightly on the mooring line to provide tension to the aft lines holding the boat off the dock. If need be, use a rolling hitch knot from a spare line onto the mooring line and run the spare line back through a winch. Make fast the mooring line so that it is taut. Depower the engine. Make adjustments all around and run the plank off the stern of the boat to the quay. Take a big breath and exhale slowly.

Med Mooring with an anchor

This is often done in Greece. The first few times you do this, you will screw it up, so it's imperative you practice. It's not hard. You just need some good coordination between the helmsperson and the bowperson.

You first need a bowperson who is switched on. They have to be able to let out the anchor rode at the same rate that the boat is reversing. If they do it too slowly, they can bring the boat to a stop, with all the issues of prop walk and windage immediately following. And if they do it too fast, they will just pile all the chain on the bottom. About 3 feet (1 meter) per second is a good average rate to have them pay out the anchor rode because that is about the rate the skipper will be backing. The bow person has several things to monitor: the rate of water moving under the boat, the skipper for signals, how close the boat is to the dock, and the angle that the rode is heading to the bottom. If the rode is at an angle toward the anchor, it should be payed out faster or you might be starting to drag the anchor across the bottom. That'd be bad!

You first need to position your boat so you are dropping the anchor in the right place. Consider the wind direction and prop walk. In high winds, you need your boat moving backwards to overcome windage and you need to maintain your reverse direction towards the dock. It is very important that you drop your anchor with plenty of scope. Given the complexity of the maneuver, you cannot afford to have the anchor drag. More scope is better, but balance that with not running out of available rode 10 feet (3 meters) before the quay. That would suck!

Once the stern is set to the quay, the helmsperson applies forward thrust and rudder angle, if needed, to stabilize the boat with the wind. The anchorperson then tightens up on the anchor to hold the boat off the quay.

Wind direction will determine your plan.

Into the Wind

Backing up into the wind toward the quay is easiest. Drop the anchor and use your expert backing skills to bring the boat home. The anchorperson doesn't have too much responsibility other than to not stop the boat with the anchor and make sure the anchor is not being dragged in as the boat backs. (i.e. not too much but not too little rode is going out).

In a Crosswind

It is similar with a crosswind. The idea is to get the boat in as fast as possible to the quay, keeping it moving to get to the dock. The helmsperson might need to ferry the boat in the wind to counteract the leeway. More than likely you are going to be skewed off and pushed downwind. For this reason, prepare a long spring line from a windward amidships cleat and get it ashore and tied directly to a quay cleat as soon as possible. Now you can use rudder and forward thrust to straighten your boat out as well as spring it upwind.

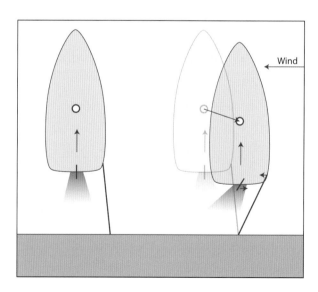

Downwind

Backing downwind is also easy, but requires a different plan. First, get the anchor dug in and set so that, at one boat length out, the helmsperson can start to relinquish control to the anchorperson. The helmsperson applies slight reverse thrust and the anchorperson now lets out the rode 3 feet (1 meter) at a time to allow the boat to drop back into position. At about 3 feet from the quay wall, the anchorperson holds while the reverse thrust is maintained. The stern lines are made taut and reverse thrust is stopped.

Other Med Mooring points to consider

If you are going to do a Med Mooring with an anchor, make really sure that for this marina, anchoring is the way you're supposed to do it. Because if you do it in a marina where there are other cables laid across the bottom holding docks and sunken mooring blocks in place, you *will definitely* get your anchor hooked on these. The absolute last thing in the world you want to do is to swim in a Mediterranean marina. Many boats in the Mediterranean pump out their heads directly into the ocean and you *will definitely* come down with a nasty disease.

To gauge the point where to drop the anchor, use the boat length as the gauge for distance. If you want 120 feet of rode out and if you have a 40-foot boat, then use three boat lengths as the point where you want the anchor to lie. But also make sure the bowman allows time for the anchor to fall to the bottom.

The key here is practice. Work with the bowperson to show how to deploy the anchor rode at the desirable rate.

You can do this practice anywhere—*just* don't do it for the first time in the marina with a crosswind and traffic and million dollar boats all around. Practice!

Med Mooring debrief

At the end of every Med Mooring event that you do on your vacation with your relatively green landlubber crew, good or bad, do a debrief on how you all could have done it better and what to do next time. Remember to keep your "good-leader" hat on. Take the blame and responsibility upon yourself first—that you could have given better instructions or your did not anticipate that.

The Perfect Landing

In a little Greek port called Perdika, just southwest of Athens, we Med-Moored up to the quay at about 9:00 one morning. We'd just come from Aegina and decided we needed another coffee. Throughout our maneuver, the guy in the boat next to our intended parking spot kept eating his cereal from a bowl while watching and reading a book. A testament to a perfect landing.

A Not-So-Perfect Landing

A few days later in Poros, we did not set the anchor out far enough in a strong crosswind. I asked the anchor-person to tighten up on the anchor because we were bow-down in the wind and had not set a windward spring line and the person on the dock tied the aft line to a leeward quay cleat (all my fault, by the way). After

---

a while she announced that the anchor was dangling below the bow. Whoops! As this was going on, people from everywhere had set down their drinks to help. We renamed Poros "Amateur Island" after our poorly planned and executed maneuver. Fortunately, there was no gelcoat damage—just ego damage and a good learning story aptly placed in this book.

The second time we got it right by proper preparation and using a windward amidships spring line.

Chapter 10
Catamaran Maneuvering

Introduction

Typically, people own their own monohulls and charter a cat on a vacation. If this is you, taking a big cat out of the marina is going to be your first time behind two engines spread 20 feet (6 meters) apart. That is potentially intimidating.

The question with cats is this: Can you guarantee yourself that you will get the boat back to the marina and into the slip perfectly without damage? If you're hesitant, then we recommend that once you have made it out of the harbor, you do some practicing with the teachings here. Fear not, a cat is so much more maneuverable than a monohull.

In the Caribbean, you will most likely be anchoring and mooring, so a few imprecise maneuvers during the week are no problem. But in the Mediterranean, you will need precise maneuvering skills to squeeze in beside the megayachts Med-Moored at the the quay. Regardless, when you bring the cat back to base you'd better be practiced. You'll need to dock it perfectly at the fuel dock, and it might be a tight squeeze.

Note, however, if you're ever uncomfortable in any chartering situation doing your final docking, just call the charter company on VHF and have them send out a chase boat with a captain to dock the boat for you. There is no shame, and the charter company appreciates it.

Getting the General Feel

Some have compared maneuvering a cat with driving a bulldozer. Well . . . perhaps!

Chances are, you have not driven a real bulldozer but you do remember your childhood sandbox. The tracks on each side of the bulldozer move independently to allow the bulldozer to do some amazing maneuvering. A cat has the same ability. The two propellers on the cat are mounted at the aft end of each hull, placing the thrust forces far apart. This greatly enhances the turning moment. The throttles on the two engines, therefore, have the same maneuvering effect as the levers on a bulldozer. Push one forward and the other in reverse and the cat will spin on itself.

If you can imagine a bulldozer, when you push the left track lever forward and the right track lever backward, which way does the bulldozer spin? Clockwise right? The left track goes forward and the right track goes back; this acts to turn the bulldozer clockwise.

- Both tracks forwards—bulldozer goes forward.
- Both tracks back—bulldozer goes backward.

- Left track back and right track forward—bulldozer turns counterclockwise.
- Right track back and left track forward—bulldozer turns clockwise.

And bulldozers are cool because they can turn inside their own length. So again cats are exactly the same. With the wheel locked in the center, try this:

- Both throttles forward—cat goes forward.
- Both throttles back—cat goes backward.
- Left throttle back and right throttle forward—cat spins counterclockwise.
- Right throttle back and left throttle forward—cat spins clockwise
- Left throttle back a little and right throttle forward full—slow forward turn counterclockwise.
- Right throttle back a little and left throttle forwards full—slow forward turn clockwise.

Scan the QR code to play with the animation by clicking on the arrows. Note that for broad turning, the reverse throttle is not all the way back.

There are some other cool things you can do too.

Wheel to port: Port throttle forward and starboard throttle slightly back will vector the boat sideways to starboard. Watch the water thrust over the port rudder. There is no water over the starboard rudder because that engine is in reverse.

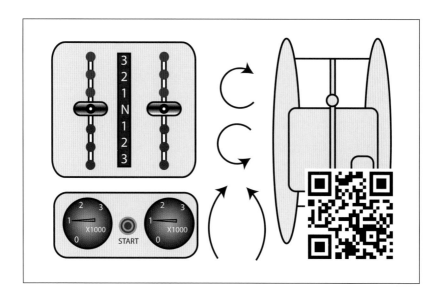

The principle here is that the boat wants to spin clockwise but the thrust on the rudder is pushing the stern of the boat to starboard. Thus, the effect vectors the boat sideways.

And as seen in the animation above, cats can turn inside their own length. They are the ultimate maneuvering boat. So next time you're thinking about being intimidated by the beam and sheer size of the cat, think about how much more maneuverable the cat is. *But* . . . it takes practice and learned intuition on which throttles to use.

As ridiculous as it seems, we want you to get into your favorite armchair right now, clench your fists around a couple of big screwdrivers, and practice moving those bulldozer levers alternately left-back/right-forward and vice versa. (Feel free to make *brrrmmmbrrrmmm* noises.) You'll intuitively feel which way the bulldozer will turn. Do it a couple of dozen times and you've probably got enough skill to get you out of the marina—barely.

Practice all the monohull examples given in this book on your cat once you're out of the marina, clear of everyone, clear of sight of the charter company and before you set the sails. Also do the following maneuvers:

- Spin the boat clockwise.
- Spin the boat counterclockwise.
- Vector the boat sideways.
- Engage just one throttle in forward and see what the boat does.
- Engage just one throttle in reverse and see what the boat does.
- Wheel hard over to port and both throttle forward.
- Wheel hard over to port and engage both throttles in reverse.

There is a temptation to forget about the rudders when maneuvering because the engines are extremely effective.

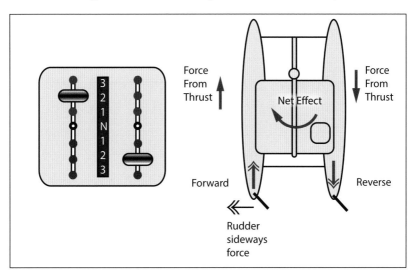

But remember from monohull maneuvering that the rudders are also very effective. So be cognizant of the rudders. For example, if you want to rotate the boat in a clockwise direction (bow to starboard, stern to port) then turn the wheel to starboard. The starboard reverse engine will not have an effect on the rudder but the port forward engine will push the stern to port, increasing the rate of turn.

If you accidently had the rudders turned the other way, to port, you will automatically and unnecessarily have a reduced turning effect.

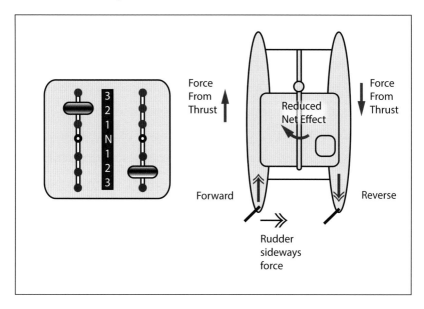

Now try backing the boat with the wind coming from forward. The wind will want to push the front of the boat downwind, but you can compensate by adjusting the throttle to keep the cat moving straight back.

The next thing to become confident about is how quickly or slowly the boat will stop. You'll notice that the forward momentum of the boat is hard to quell with the engines.

This is because the propellers are set up to be efficient in forward thrust, but not in reverse thrust. Thus, significant understanding of killing off boat momentum should be practiced—away from anything. You'll be surprised how long it takes some of these boats to stop. No problem, however; you're gaining the feel with all the exercises above. In reverse, the story is different. Reverse momentum, as with a monohull, can be killed off quickly with just a little (efficient) forward thrust.

Discovering the general maneuverability of the boat away from the dock and marina is important, not just for reducing embarrassment, but for your credit card deposit or insurance deductibles. Collisions in boats this expensive are simply unnecessary when you've spent a little time practicing and gaining an appreciation of the maneuverability of the boat. Essentially you are learning the feel of the boat. Don't be embarrassed—it's much more embarrassing to even put a little scratch in the gelcoat in front of the charter office upon return. And besides, it's fun to learn the maneuverability of the boat.

Prop walk

Prop walk problems? Nope! In a monohull, the boat will pull to port when engaging in reverse, and there is really not too much that you can do about it. In a catamaran, the same will happen except, cleverly, we'll engage the port engine in reverse a little more than the starboard engine. This creates a counterclockwise moment that overcomes the clockwise moment of prop walk. If you're having trouble visualizing this, remember that port engine in reverse and starboard in forward creates a huge counterclockwise moment. In a similar fashion, less starboard engine than port will still create a (much smaller) counterclockwise moment. In reality, you probably won't notice it because you automatically adjust the throttle positions to get the boat moving straight backward.

Ferrying

A cat can ferry perpendicular to the wind or current in the same manner as a monohull, except it has far more capability to accurately angle itself perfectly to the wind and current flow. Refer to the ferrying example and animation earlier in Chapter 8.

Getting off the dock

Because the cat has the ability to spin on its own axis, rarely will you need to use spring lines to gain a turning moment. But there is also nothing preventing you from utilizing spring lines. They work the same as they do for a monohull.

In the situation below, you are tied starboard side to the dock with a boat in front of you and another one behind you. The trick is going to be to pivot your catamaran to either move the bow clear of the catamaran in front or the stern clear of the catamaran behind you.

The best maneuver depends on the winds and currents, of course. This is going to be easier than a monohull because of the improved maneuverability of the catamaran. If the wind is coming from ahead or blowing you off, clear the bow first with or without a spring line, whichever you are comfortable with and depending on the wind strength.

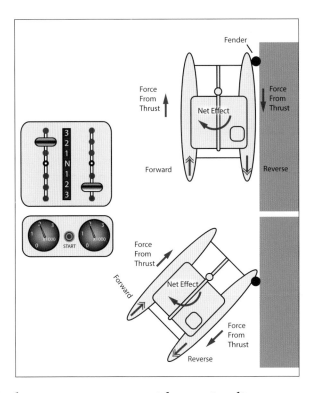

Here is the same maneuver with a spring line.

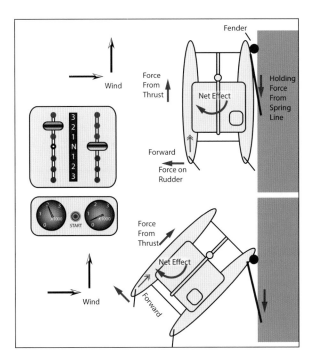

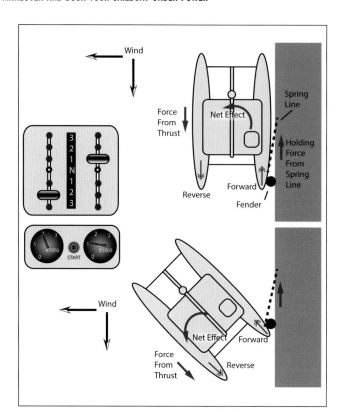

To start:

- Make your plan.
- Inform the crew of the procedure and assign tasks.
- Check for obstacles in the water.
- Ensure the dinghy is clear.
- Ensure no lines are in the water.
- Check for traffic.

In the animation below, the wind is blowing you either into the dock or is behind. Note that since we are using both engines (one in reverse) you can probably get away without using a spring line.

Tap the QR code to play the animation showing a cat using opposing thrust to turn itself off a dock.

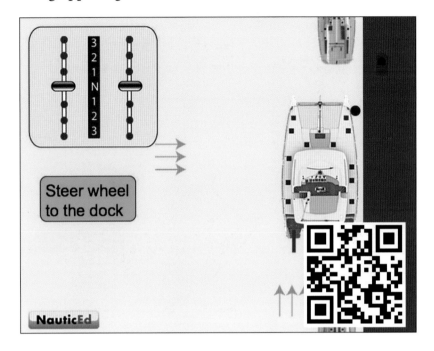

The animation below shows the same situation but for winds from ahead or blowing you off the dock. Here you're only using the outer engine in reverse, so rig a spring line from aft to forward on the dock. The main reason is there is reduced maneuverability because there is no wash over the rudder and we don't have a counter opposing forward thrust. Thus, the spring line acts to prevent the boat moving backwards.

Once you have cleared the boats around you, you can then bring the throttles back to neutral. At that point, if you need to turn around to go in the other direction, wait for your boat to stabilize and then engage one of the throttles in

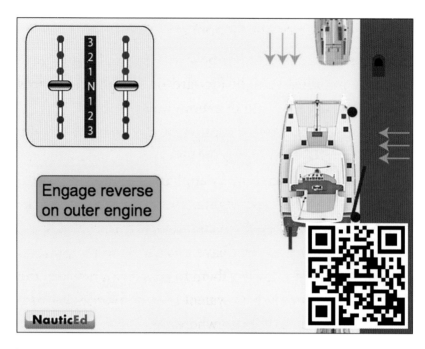

one direction and the other throttle in the other direction and your catamaran should start to pivot.

You will also need to use a spring line to spring a cat upwind in a Med Mooring situation. Use an amidships spring line with wheel turned to leeward and forward thrust.

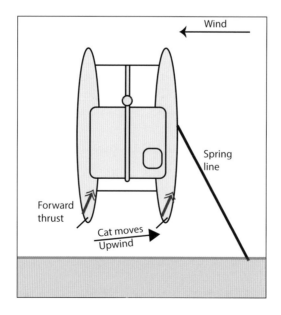

Leaving the slip or Med Mooring

If you are parked stern to or bow in, you would then leave the dock in either straight forward or straight backwards motion just as you would in a monohull.

In a straight backward motion, you're going to feel the effects of prop walk dragging the aft to port. Unlike a monohull, this is easily overcome by applying slightly less reverse throttle on the starboard engine. This creates an anticlockwise turning moment, which counteracts the prop walk.

Somehow, because you have a cat, it is so tempting to run things over by allowing them to pass down between the hulls. This is particularly prevalent in tight marinas because there are mooring balls everywhere.

1. Try not to do it. There are pendants semi-floating next to a mooring ball.
2. If you have to do it, disengage your gearing to prevent the prop catching the pendant as you pass.

Coming back to the dock

Using the exercises described in the maneuvering section of this book, you'll simply be able to maneuver your cat into position, spin it around using both engines, and back into or drive into position.

While the wind will want to push your boat sideways, you always have control of the boat with both engines.

Depending on wind, however, you may need to spring on. You can use exactly the same methods as for a monohull described earlier.

Vectoring the last few feet to the dock can be achieved with the correct combination of thrust and rudder. View this animation.

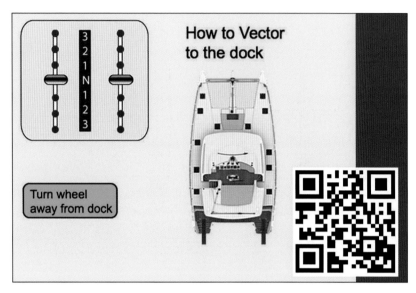

If there are higher wind and current situations, just remember that since the cat can spin on its own diameter, you can always abort whatever you are attempting and have another go from a different angle. Going around for a second pass is far less embarrassing than swapping gelcoat with another boat.

Tying up

If you are side to the dock, you can tie the non-dockside hulls to the dock in this manner. This provides for plenty of spring stretch in the lines, but holds the boat to the dock.

If you are docking your catamaran stern to the dock, you can cross in an "X" two dock lines on the stern of the boat.

The point is to tie lines as long as possible to allow for a spring stretch in the lines but to hold the boat in position.

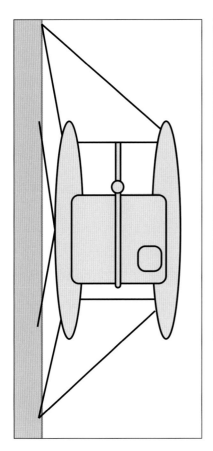
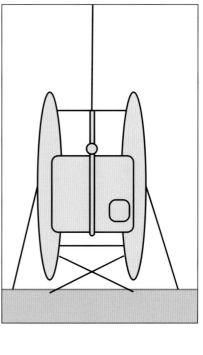

Catamaran Maneuvering Summary

While the giant size of a catamaran can seem intimidating, from the skills learned here you can see that, with a cat, you can overcome about any maneuverability problem.

If you can handle your monohull, you will have far less stress in any maneuvering situation with a cat.

We can't stress enough, however, that you must get the feel for the maneuverability out in open water where you can't hit anything. In the marina is *not* the place to practice. We've given you the principles here, but the only real way to "get it" is to try it.

CatNed, the Maneuvering Game

And now, we'd like to introduce you to CatNed, our Maneuvering a Catamaran Under Power Interactive and Educational Game. Unfortunately, CatNed is built using Flash-based gaming technology, so it does not work on mobile devices. Never fear, CatNed is free to play online. Go to NauticEd.org and sign up for a free account. Once logged in, on the myCurriculum page you will see free games at the bottom right of the page. You'll need to do this on a computer—a Mac or PC is ok—just not a mobile device.

We highly recommend that you play the game. You will gain a real appreciation for maneuvering with the opposing throttles. You'll be turning and backing the boat into slips all the while being yelled at by the port authority in strange languages and accents to not park here but over there (which is usually the case in a foreign port).

Conclusion

Well that's it! You're an expert, right? Not! Because you haven't yet gone out and done it and practiced it and practiced it again.

Here is what to do next: check the forecast for a gorgeous windy day that is upcoming. Then call a friend and coax him or her into coming out for a practice training session. On the day, make some sandwiches, grab a few libations (non-alcoholic), and head out. Take this book and go through all the exercises.

We guarantee you'll have a great and memorable day with your friend.